THE
SPUR BOOK
OF
KNOTS

Send for a list of
SPUR FOOTPATH GUIDES

Walks Along the South Downs Way
Walks in Hertfordshire
Walks Along the Ridgeway
Walks in the New Forest
Round Walks West of London
Chiltern Round Walks
Walks in the Surrey Hills
Walks in the Thameside Chilterns
Dorset Walks
Walks in South Essex
Afoot in Essex Again

Venture Guides titles include:
   Knots, Bonds & Hitches
   Map & Compass
   Camping
   Basic Sailing
   Snorkelling
   Weather Lore
   Outdoor First Aid
   Survival and Rescue

THE
SPUR BOOK
OF
KNOTS

by

Terry Brown & Rob Hunter

SPURBOOKS LIMITED

Published by Spurbooks Ltd

6 Parade Court
Bourne End
Bucks

ISBN 0 902875 96 5

Printed by Maund & Irvine, Ltd. Tring, Herts.

CONTENTS

THE KNOTS

These are in alphabetical order for reference.
To learn from scratch, begin at the beginning.

WHIPPING AND SPLICING

INTRODUCTION

Ropes and cordage, knots, bends and hitches, present an evocative vision to the layman. There is something rugged and romantic about the ability to handle rope, and tie a useful knot.

Moreover, increasingly in recent years, the return of vast numbers of people to outdoor pursuits, to sailing, climbing, camping and rambling, has led to a need for information on suitable knots for a variety of purposes.

THE USE AND PURPOSE OF THIS BOOK

There exists an exhaustive library of books on this subject, many illustrating literally hundreds of knots, most of which are of no use whatsoever to people following outdoor pursuits. Others, of more practical application, have illustrations so small, or descriptions so vague, that little benefit can be obtained from them.

Our purpose here, has been to list some thirty knots, directly relevant to the activities of climbers, campers, yachtsmen and ramblers, even to those who only want to tie up a parcel.

Once selected, we have illustrated the knots with large, clear drawings, and step by step instructions, with the minimum of jargon, and finally tested text and drawings on the least practical people we could find—our wives.

HOW TO LEARN KNOT-TYING

For practise at home, desk or club, (and this book is designed for learning knot-tying *before* the need arises), we recommend the use of at least nine feet of half inch diameter nylon or terylene rope, available very cheaply from sports shops or ship chandlers. Two lengths will be necessary to practise some of the knots, for example, the Prusik Knot.

Knot-tying is great fun, and must be one of the most useful and inexpensive pastimes you can possibly find. At home, a chair back or table leg will provide an adequate substitute for a spar, mast or bollard, or as a securing point for the climbing knots. All the instructions have been written with this in mind, and assume that the reader is right handed. A little trial and error will quickly reveal how the left handed person can adapt the instructions.

ROPES AND CORDAGE

These words cover a wide range of materials for use in various forms of outdoor activities.

Until quite recently, most ropes and cordage came from natural fibres, sisal, manila, hemp or cotton. Nowadays, these fibres have been almost totally replaced by man-made fibres such as nylon or terylene.

These man-made fibres are generally superior to their natural predecessors, being lighter, stronger, less prone to rot, and water resistant. It can be accepted therefore, that for most purposes man-made fibres are the most suitable and readily available.

It is most important to have the right rope for the

particular task. Equally, it is no good wishing to know a knot when you are stuck half way up a cliff or are out in a Force 8 gale. Learn these knots before you need them.

Nylon ropes for climbers, or terylene ropes which float for sailors, are most suitable and require little maintenance. The range of fibres, ropes and cordage is vast, and the sportsman is advised to consult a competent stockist and listen carefully to his advice on the best rope necessary for the task in hand.

Good ropes and cordage are not cheap, but they are much cheaper than a broken bone or a new mast.

CARE OF ROPES AND CORDAGE

Dirt is the great enemy of cordage. It works its way into the fibres and saws away at them, gradually weakening the material until it frays and snaps.

Ropes should be kept out of the dirt, never trodden on or trampled underfoot, and sluiced clean of grime with clear, fresh, water if and when they get dirty. Once wet they should be allowed to dry slowly in a dry place—not in front of a stove or fire. Coiled neatly, they should be hung up ready for future use. Periodic testing two or three times a season is advisable, and at the slightest sign of wear, the rope should be replaced. In the end this is cheaper than a major accident.

Knots, themselves, weaken ropes. If a rope is knotted, the strength near the knot is reduced by about fifty percent, and this should be borne in mind as a safety factor on load-bearing ropes. Finally, remember that knot-tying is a manipulative skill and can only be kept in existence by regular practise.

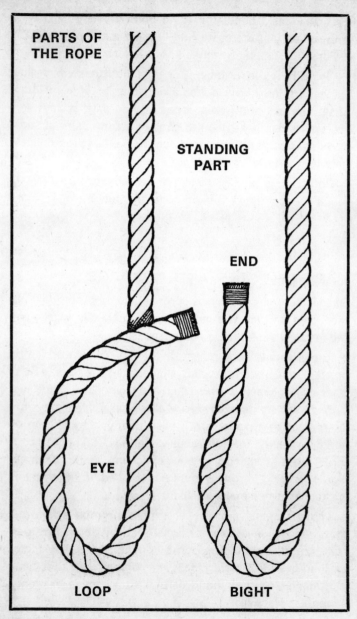

PARTS OF THE ROPE

STANDING PART

END

EYE

LOOP

BIGHT

SOME SIMPLE DEFINITIONS

If we accept the term "Knot" as the general word for a fastening made with cordage, the following are more precise terms, frequently employed in the names of knots, and a guide to their particular function. You must understand these terms if you are to follow the instructions for tying which follow.

(1) The *Standing part* is the main part of the rope, above a loop or bight. It is the part opposed to the *end*.

(2) The *end* is, as the term implies, the end or unsecured part of the rope.

(3) A *bight* is a half, or open circle in a rope and also refers to the middle part of a length of rope.

(4) A *loop* is a closed circle in a rope.

(5) A *Knot* in the precise meaning of the term, is any knot, other than a bend or hitch! The best known knots are "stopping" knots, such as the Figure of Eight knot, which is used to prevent the rope running out through a cleat or fairlead.

(6) A *bend* is the knot used for tying one rope to another.

(7) A *hitch* is used for fastening a rope to another object, such as a spar, or tent peg.

Readers should note that two of the knots in this book, the Fisherman's Bend and Stuns'l Bend, though called bends, are actually hitches. Knotting terms are open to a variety of interpretations but we believe these are generally correct and certainly apply to the instructions in this book.

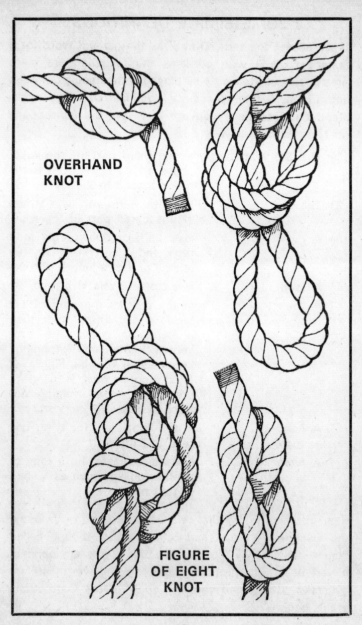

OVERHAND KNOT

FIGURE OF EIGHT KNOT

OVERHAND OR THUMB KNOT

Uses: This is a "stopper" knot and well enough known to be used unconsciously by practically everybody for a range of purposes from tying up parcels to putting a loop in a climbing rope. It is the most basic of knots. A better one for stopping ropes is the Figure of Eight Knot.

How to tie: Take the rope in the left hand and form a loop by laying the end across the face of the standing part. Tuck the end round the rope and back through the loop, and pull tight to form the knot.

FIGURE OF EIGHT KNOT

Uses: This is a "stopper" knot, used to stop a rope running out through a cleat, block or fairlead. It has the big advantage of being easy to untie, and is useful in stopping a frayed rope from unravelling further.

How to tie: This knot is tied in the end of the rope. Take the rope in the left hand, and form a loop by laying the end across the face of the standing part. Then lead the end round the back of the standing part and down, through the front of the loop. When the end is pulled, the rope falls into the figure of eight shape, from which the knot takes its name, and a stopper knot is formed. This knot is easier to undo than the overhand knot.

FISHERMAN'S KNOT

REEF KNOT

FISHERMAN'S KNOT (OR WATER-KNOT)

Uses: This is a popular knot with climbers, for joining two ends of a sling, and an excellent safe knot for joining together two ropes of equal thickness, especially if they are not too bulky. Fishermen use it for tying gut, or thin line—it is sometimes called the Angler's Knot. It should not be used for tying together climbing ropes.

How to tie: Lay the two ends side by side. Then, taking one end, tie an overhand knot around the standing part of the other rope. Then repeat the process with the other end and standing part. Then pull on the standing part of both ropes, and the two overhand knots will slide together, to form the knot.

THE REEF KNOT

Uses: This is a popular and widely used knot, generally employed for tying together two ends of the same rope, as when reefing a sail—hence the name; or tying a parcel.

As it lies flat, it is used in first-aid, for tying a sling or bandage. Climbers can use it for tying their waist lines. The great feature of the reef knot is that it will not jam and is easy to untie. It should not be used when the strain on the knot comes at an angle.

How to tie: Take one end in either hand, and tie left over right and under; then right over left and under. Then, holding the ends and standing parts, pull tight.

Note the overhand sequence *carefully*. If you tie this knot incorrectly, you will tie a "granny" knot, which is dangerous. A "granny" knot will not lie flat, and so is easily detected.

SHEET
BEND

DOUBLE
SHEET
BEND

SHEET BEND

Uses: This knot, like most bends, is used for joining two ropes together. The single sheet bend is used for joining two ropes of equal thickness. It can also be used for securing a rope to the eye of a cable or hawser.

How to tie: Take one rope, form a loop in the end and hold in the left hand. With the right hand put the end of the other rope through the loop from behind. Then up and round the back of the doubled rope, then across the face of the loop, tucking the end under itself and over the face of the loop. Then pull tight.

Be sure you have both ends on the same side of the knot, otherwise you have formed an unsafe "Left Hand Sheet Bend".

DOUBLE SHEET BEND

Uses: This is a more secure version of the Sheet Bend. Use it in place of the Sheet Bend for two ropes of *unequal* thickness, or for greater security.

How to tie: Form a loop in the thicker rope. In all cases, when joining two ropes of unequal thickness together, the loop goes in the thicker one.

Take the loop in the left hand. Lead the other end through the loop from behind, and around the neck of the loop *twice.* On the first turn be sure the end goes *under* itself, then round the neck, back, tucking under itself and across the bight. Pull tight. Check that both ends are on the same side of the knot.

BOWLINE

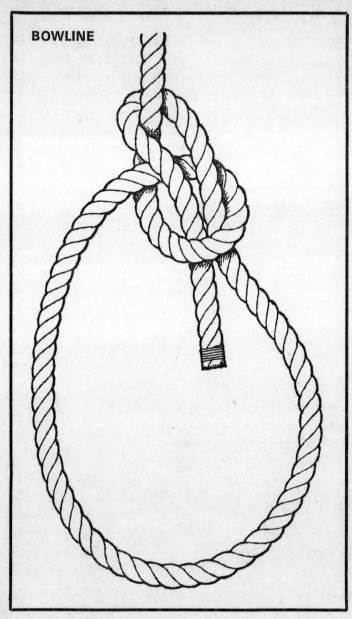

THE BOWLINE

Uses: This is the queen of knots, with a wide range of uses. The basic purpose is to put a non-slip knot in a rope, and thus form an eye, bight or loop. It can be used for making a waist loop or for securing a mooring line, or for putting a haulage loop in the rope's end. Climbers should secure the bowline with an overhand knot—indeed, they should so secure all their knots.

The Bowline has a large number of variations but the basic jack-of-all-trades knot is tied as follows.

How to tie: This is the simplest method we know. Many people advise learning the Bowline by tying the rope round your waist. The snag is that after a while that becomes the only way you can tie it. One yachtsman we know, ties the Bowline around his waist, then wriggles out of the loop, and drops it over the bollard. He's been doing that since 1941. Why not try it this way.

Hold the rope in the left hand and form a small loop over the top of the standing part.

Hold in place with the thumb of the left hand. Then lead the end through the back of the loop, round behind the standing part, and tuck the end back through the loop. Pull tight and presto!

It is possible, with practise, and a degree of manual dexterity, to tie this knot with one hand, a useful trick for climbers. Many Scouts were taught and remember this knot with the tale that "the rabbit comes up out of the hole (the loop), round the tree (the standing part), and back down the hole!"

BOWLINE ON THE BIGHT

BOWLINE ON THE BIGHT

Uses: If you need a secure loop, you can use a Bowline. If you need a *double* loop, then a useful knot to tie is the Bowline on the Bight. This can be used for hauling or lowering a man up or down a cliff or ship's side, either with one leg through each loop, and holding the standing part, or with one loop under the arms, and the other round the hips. If the loops are of equal size, the knot gives extra security to a mooring, or can be used to secure the rope over the two points, for example, a tent guy-rope can be secured over two tent pegs, for extra security in high winds.

How to tie: This is a knot that needs to be worked into shape. Double the end up the standing part to make a good long bight, and take the doubled rope in your left hand. Using the doubled rope, form a loop at the top, as in the ordinary Bowline, and feed the main bight up through the loop from behind, until you have as much of the bight above the loop as below it.

This is the tricky part. Take hold of the upper bight and bring it down, over and behind, the lower loop.

This will give you two lower loops. Holding the knot in place, pull on the loops until the knot is tight.

This is a simple knot to tie once you have the knack, but be sure to start with a good, long, bight.

**TRIPLE
BOWLINE**

TRIPLE BOWLINE

Uses: This is used to form *three* loops in a rope. The uses are similar to those of the Bowline on the Bight, although the Triple Bowline is easier to tie, unless the rope is very thick. It is a good, safe knot, for lowering an unconscious person, with two long thigh loops, and a shorter chest loop.

How to tie: Quite simply, the Triple Bowline is tied in exactly the same way as the ordinary Bowline, but using a doubled rope to give *three* loops.

Hold the doubled rope in the left hand, form a loop at the top and feed the end of the bight through. then proceed as for the ordinary Bowline. Assuming that you want three equal loops, be sure to work the ends evenly, and start with a good long length of doubled rope.

RUNNING BOWLINE

RUNNING BOWLINE

Uses: If you need to have a running noose, and can only tie the Bowline, then this is the knot for you. Unlike the other Bowlines, this should never be tied around the person, or you will end up in two halves!

How to tie: The Running Bowline is formed by tying a Bowline, with a small eye, in the end of the rope, and then feeding the other end through the eye to form the running noose.

Alternatively, if there is too much rope to feed through the loop, tie a Bowline, as above, and pull the standing part through the eye until you have sufficient rope for the noose.

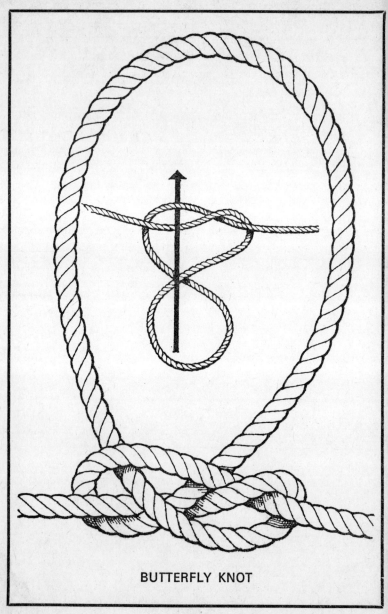

BUTTERFLY KNOT

ALPINE BUTTERFLY
(or BUTTERFLY, or ARTILLERY KNOT)

Uses: This again is a climbing knot, and used for putting a fixed loop in the middle of a rope, when you are unable to use the ends.

How to tie: Form a loop with the bottom towards you and the rope crossed at the top. Taking the standing part of the underneath rope, and fold back over the loop, to form a smaller half bight. Then twist the main loop to make a figure of eight shape.

Then take the bottom of the main loop and feed through the small loop at the top, under the top of the main loop, and pull through, to form the Butterfly Knot.

PRUSIK KNOT

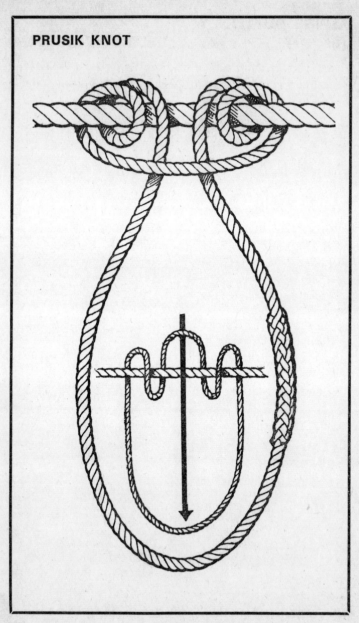

PRUSIK KNOT

Uses: This is a climbing knot, and generally used for attaching a sling to a standing rope. As it will grip the standing rope by friction, and also slide along, it can be used for rescue work, or for climbing up the rope on an overhang. Yachtsmen can use it to climb the shrouds, or to shin up a rope to clear the halyards.

The unique feature of this knot is that, while it can easily be slid along the standing rope, it will grip firmly if a sudden strain or jerk is put upon it. It works rather like a seat belt in a car.

How to tie: For this you will need two lengths of rope. In climbing, the knot is usually tied with a closed sling. To practise tying this knot, tie the main rope, to which you will attach the sling, securely at both ends. Although a sling is usual, the knot can be learned with a looped rope.

Take the sling or loop and pass a bight underneath the main rope. Bring this bight back over the main rope, through the middle of the sling and back under the main rope.

Then take the upper end of the sling, and poke it across the main rope, and through the lower loop. Give the sling a sharp jerk and it will remain immovable but it will slide freely, if you push it along.

TARBUCK KNOT

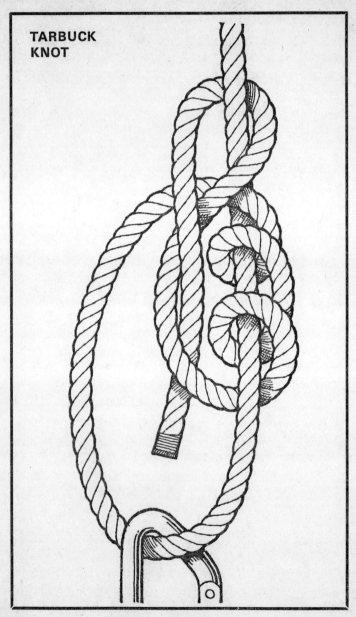

TARBUCK KNOT

Uses: This is a climbing knot, one of the few to bear the name of the man who developed it, in this case Ken Tarbuck. It is a friction knot, and is useful for the cushioning effect it has, for, if a sudden strain falls on a waist line or Karabiner, it will give slowly, taking up the strain.

Primarily it is used to fasten a waist line to the main rope while climbing. It can also be used on tent guy ropes, for with this knot the grip will automatically slacken as it is tightened elsewhere. As the drawing indicates, it is a loop knot, designed to be tied round something else, such as a waist line or Karabiner.

How to tie: Extend the rope at right angles away from your body, and lead the end through the Karabiner, and back up, to make *three* turns round the standing part, down the rope towards you. Keeping the loop of the bight to the left and these three turns completed, lead the end up, above the turns, across and round behind the standing part and back down, tucking the end back under itself (see diagram). Make sure the knot is tight. This knot is designed specifically for nylon ropes. For safety, when leading, the knot should be kept at least a foot away from the Karabiner.

HONDA KNOT

HONDA KNOT

Uses: This is the knot for fireside cowboys, used for making a lasso. It produces a fine circular knot and loop. If, as a child, after a visit to the circus, you went home to try some rope spinning and found that you couldn't make a clean loop, you were probably using a different knot. This is the correct one. Try it, and impress the kids!

How to tie: Hold the rope with the end in your right hand. With the left hand, form a half hitch in the standing part. With the right hand, make a bight in the rope and feed this through the half hitch, thus forming an eye. Now put an overhand knot in the end, to prevent it running through the half hitch, then pull the eye tight. Feed the other end through the eye thus formed, and you have a lasso.

If you form the half hitch on the wrong side of the rope, the knot will fall apart. Simply form the half hitch on the other side, and you will find it holds.

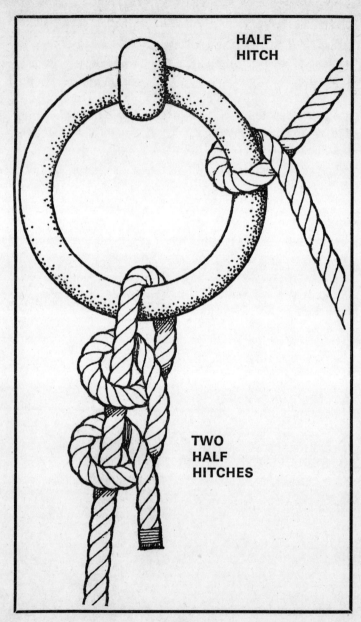

HALF HITCH

TWO HALF HITCHES

34

HALF HITCH

Uses: The Half Hitch in itself is hardly a knot at all. Nevertheless, as we shall see, it forms a part of many other knots, and must therefore be clearly understood as a basic component of other knots. A Half Hitch will only work if it jams against its own standing part.

How to tie: This is very simple. Feed the rope through or round an object, and cross over, until the ropes bear against each other.

TWO HALF HITCHES

Uses: This is commonly used to secure a boat to a mooring ring. Basically, it is a quick securing knot, suitable for a brief stop, such as going through a lock or for a short stay at a quay. It can be used instead of an Overhand Knot to secure climbing knots on a waist-band.

How to tie: Take a bight round or through or over the mooring point. Pass the end around the standing part and through the loop thus formed, for the first half hitch. Then repeat the process.

Ease the knot up against the securing point. Be sure you have a long end free, to hold the hitches in position.

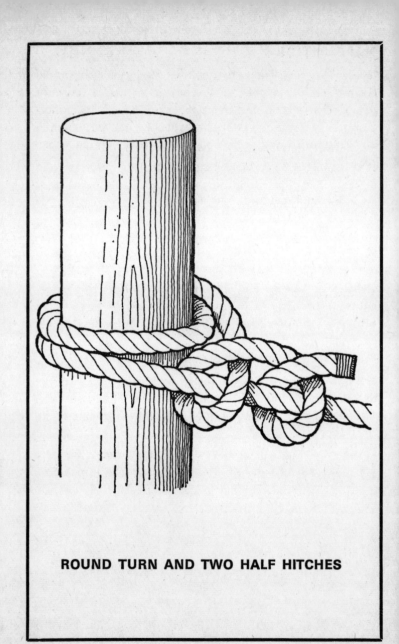

ROUND TURN AND TWO HALF HITCHES

ROUND TURN AND TWO HALF HITCHES

Uses: This is a very secure knot, combining obviously, the Round Turn and Two Half Hitches. It can and should be used to secure a boat when leaving it for an extended period, or for greater security. It is also a good haulage knot for climbers, or for securing tent guys. The great advantage over the Fisherman's Bend is that this knot is easier to cast off.

How to tie: Remember that to make a round turn, you put the rope round your secure point *twice*, once to get the rope round anyway, and then again for security. Be sure you have the rope round twice. Then put two half hitches round the standing part. Study the drawing carefully and be sure your end goes over, and not under the rope, to start the hitch.

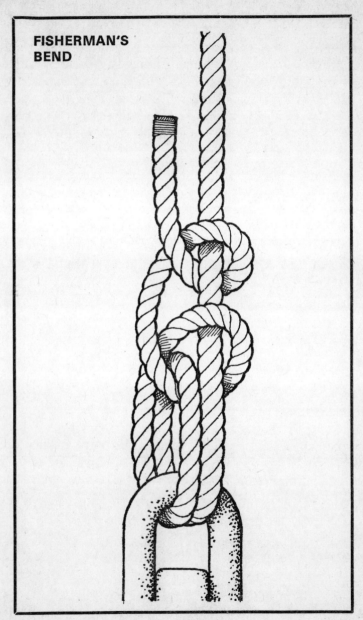

FISHERMAN'S BEND

FISHERMAN'S BEND

Uses: Please note that this is the Fisherman's Bend, *not* the Fisherman's Knot. Just to confuse matters, it is really a hitch, not a bend—see definitions. The great advantage of this knot is that it is very secure, more so than the Round Turn and Two Half Hitches, and can be used therefore, for even greater security. It should be used for bending the warp to an anchor. Because of the jamming action of this knot it is particularly useful when used with slippery synthetic rope.

How to tie: This knot is formed exactly as for the Round Turn and Two Half Hitches, *except* that the first half hitch is formed round the standing part and through the round turn.

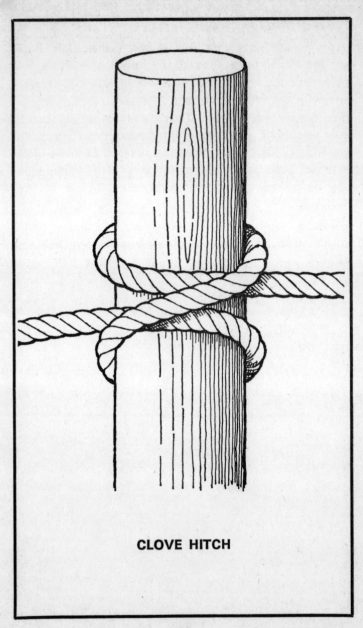

CLOVE HITCH

CLOVE HITCH

Uses: A popular use for this knot with yachtmen is to fasten the burgee-stick to the burgee halyard, thus projecting the burgee over the top of the mast. In the days of sail, this hitch was used for securing the ratlines to the shrouds. It can be used as a painter hitch.

How to tie: This knot can be tied in two ways. To tie using the middle of the rope, so that it may be placed over the securing point, form two half hitches, and place one over the other. Then drop the double loops over the bollard, or burgee-stick.

Adjust and pull tight. This hitch will slip, but if the pressure is evenly balanced on both ends, it will remain in place. When making the half hitches, be sure that one half hitch leads under the rope, and one over it.

For the second method, using the end of the rope, take a turn round the bollard or mooring point, crossing the rope over itself, then take another turn around, and lead the end through the second turn.

ROLLING HITCH

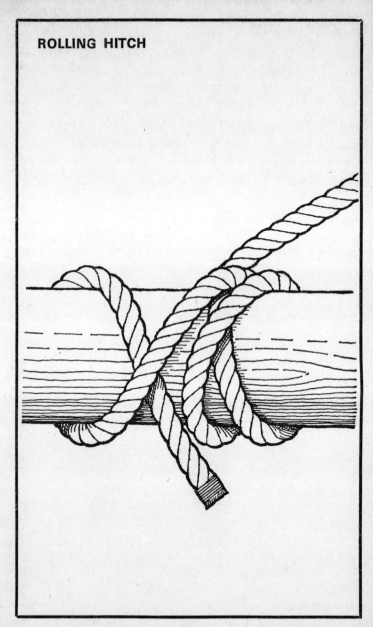

ROLLING HITCH

Uses: This is a very neat, quick and secure hitch, useful for securing a boat when the strain on the standing part of the rope, leading to the boat, comes from one side.

This is the knot to use when fastening a rope to a spar or mooring chain, and for securing a thin line to a thicker cable, for hauling. The point to remember is that you use the Rolling Hitch when the strain on the knot comes at an acute angle.

How to tie: Take two turns round the spar, across the standing part, being sure to jam the rope securely over the standing part. Then take another turn around the spar on the other side of the standing part, tucking the end under itself to make secure.

Be sure the knot is tight, and test it by jerking sharply at a sharp angle. You must start with enough rope, and have a long end to tuck away.

THAMES HITCH or TUGBOAT HITCH

THAMES HITCH or TUGBOAT HITCH

Uses: This is primarily a mooring hitch, used by lighter-men for heavy work. It is a very secure, neat hitch, and very useful for small boat sailors in securing boats to mooring posts or bollards.

How to tie: Take two turns round the mooring post with the single line, and then make a bight in the free end, and pass the bight under the standing part. Then drop the bght over the post. Pull tight. Be sure to place the turns as far down on the post or bollard as possible.

Note also that you use a single line for this hitch, not a double one.

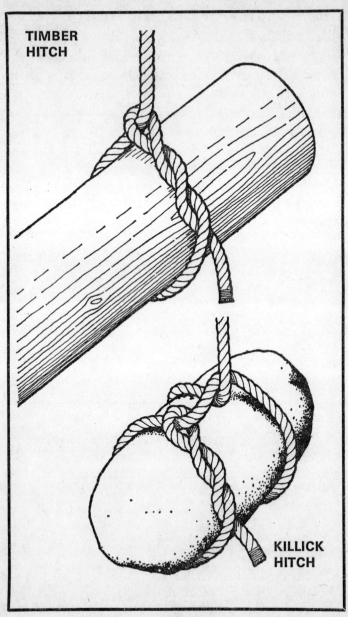

TIMBER HITCH

KILLICK HITCH

46

TIMBER HITCH

Uses: This is a very simple hitch, used as the name indicates, for towing logs out of a forest, and for similar tasks. It is, in short, a towing hitch. You can also see it used, with variations, by scaffolders. You can also use it to hoist a bale, sack or spar.

How to tie: Run the rope under the object concerned, and take the end back round the standing part. Then, with the end, take two or three turns round itself, leaving a good, long end free. It is the strain on the standing part which secures the hitch. Two or three turns round the rope are sufficient to hold it in place.

THE KILLICK HITCH

Uses: "Killick" is an old Navy term for an anchor, and the Killick Hitch is ideal for securing a heavy stone or weight to the warp, for use as an anchor, on foul ground.

How to tie: This is, quite simply, a Timber Hitch with an added half hitch, on the standing part.

MARLIN SPIKE HITCH

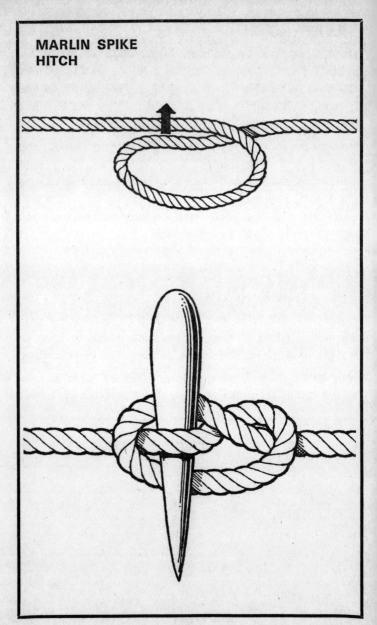

MARLIN SPIKE HITCH

Uses: This is not a securing knot, but is used for obtaining a purchase on a rope, before hauling on it. It can be used for tightening a lashing, using either a Marlin Spike, or tent peg. The spike or peg will give you purchase for hauling on the rope, and it can be used in conjunction with the Dix Knot.

How to tie: Have the rope secure at one end. Take the rope in the right hand, and make a loop in the standing part. Lay half the loop across the standing part, and then holding the rope taut, feed the Marlin Spike or tent peg through the knot. Then pull on the end and the knot will tighten around the spike, to give you a good grip.

STUNS'L BEND

Uses: This is one of a multitude of knots dating from the Age of Sail. We no longer have Stuns'ls; however, this is a good hitch for a variety of purposes. Note that although called a bend, it is in fact a hitch. This is just to confuse you.

In a gunter-rigged boat, this is commonly used for securing the gaff-halyard. Apart from this it is a good hitch for securing a rope to a spar.

How to tie: Make two turns round the spar with the end, keeping the turns to one side of the standing part. On the second turn, lead the end behind the standing part, then down, under the first and second turn, then double back, over the second turn, and finally tuck the end under the first. Pull tight.

HIGHWAYMAN'S HITCH

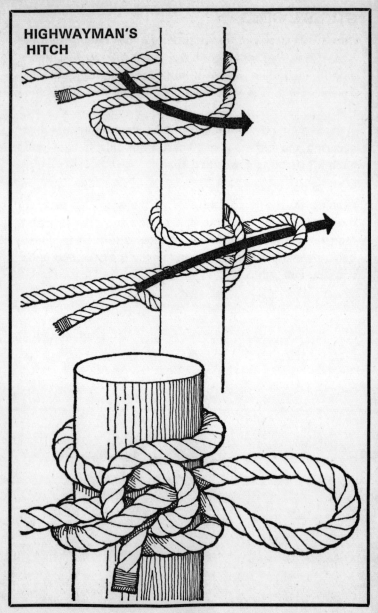

HIGHWAYMAN'S HITCH

Uses: This is a popular and clever knot for tying up a horse or securing a boat.

It is sometimes seen in Western pictures, normally when the outlaws are leaving the bank or saloon, and according to tradition gets its name by being used by Dick Turpin and other highwaymen in the 18th century. It is a quick release knot, which will stand any amount of tugging on the standing part, but will undo in a trice if the end is jerked free.

How to tie: Double the rope and run it around the securing point. Then, take the standing part, and forming a loop, pull the loop through the doubled rope.

Next, take the end, form another loop, and run this loop through the loop in the standing part. Tighten the knot by pulling on the standing part.

As you will see, the standing part is trapped by the loop of the end through the loop in the standing part.

To release the knot, jerk on the end, and the knot will collapse, and you can gallop away into the sunset.

SHEEP SHANK

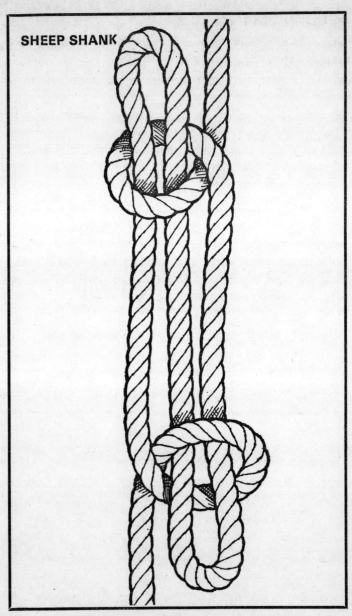

SHEEPSHANK

Uses: This is not a knot, but a method of temporarily shortening a rope, without cutting it, either to take up slack, or to pass the strain over a weakened or frayed part.

How to tie: Double the rope, to take up the required amount of slack, or to absorb the weakened part. Then make an eye in the rope at either end of the doubled section, and poke the end loop through the eyes. Pull tight.

For extra security, you can lay the end loop over the standing part at each end and insert a toggle, in the same way as for the Marlin Spike Hitch. If you have an end free, you can run it through the eye.

If desired, the rope can be doubled back and forth several times, to take up any required amount of slack.

WHIPPING AND SPLICING

When a rope is cut, the ends unravel unless they are stopped in some fashion. You can, of course, use a stopper knot, like a thumb knot or the figure of eight knot, or, with nylon ropes, just burn the ends, but it is more seaman-like and effective, to either whip the end with twine or put in a splice.

Apart from this, splicing can be used to put permanent joins or loops into your ropes.

We have shown here, in the next section, some sample whipping, and three useful splices.

WHIPPING

Uses: To put a permanent finish to a rope's end. You should use whipping twine, available from any chandlers.

There are many types of whipping, and this is the simplest.

How to do it: Take the rope and lay the twine along it for a good length, to allow for trimming, as in Fig. 1.

Then, as in Fig. 2 start binding the twine around the rope, keeping it very tight and the coils close together. You will need 12 or 13 turns for a neat whip.

When you get to the end, feed the twine end through the loop, as in Fig. 3.

Pull the other end to drag the loop and twine-end under the coils.

Then trim off the ends.

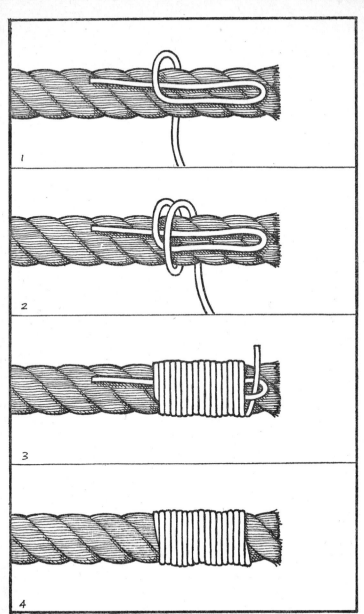

SIMPLE WHIPPING

57

BACK-SPLICE

Uses: A back-splice is a quick and permanent way of stopping a rope end unravelling and saves whipping.

Actually doing the back-splice can be difficult, unless you can do a Crown Knot (see illustrations) first.

How to do it: Unravel the rope ends for at least 6 inches, and more, depending on the thickness of the rope. Whip a piece of line or wire round the standing part to stop further unravelling. You may need to whip the end of each strand also.

Now tie the Crown Knot, (as shown in Figs. 1 to 4) and work it tight. Remove the stop-line or wire. Turn the knot upside down, with the rope away from you.

Then, take any strand, and your marlin spike. The strand goes **over** the strand goes **over** the strand in the standing part directly in front of it, and **under** the next one. Pull the end through, and then do the same with the next two strands. Always work to the left, i.e., whichever is the first strand you take, next take the one on the left, and **always** go across the lay of the rope.

Once you have woven all three strands into the rope, you start again with the first strand. You repeat the process three times and the splice is (or should be) complete.

Once you have done the Crown Knot, the rest is easy.

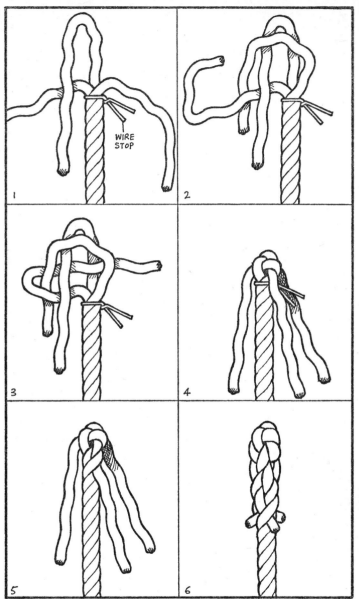

WIRE STOP

BACK SPLICE

EYE-SPLICE

Uses: To put a permanent loop in a rope, say, for mooring purposes. It is a most useful splice, but obviously it must be secure, and properly done.

How to do it: Stop the rope about 6″ from the end. Then unravel (or unlay) the rope down to this stop. Now whip the ends of the strands. Decide how big you want the eye, then make the loop, and lay unravelled ends over the standing part, at the splicing point.

Twist the standing part, or use your marlin spike, to open the strands on the standing part. Feed one strand end through (any one) and pull up to the stop.

Working to the left, take the next, left, strand and feed that **over** the strand in the standing part that has the first strand **under** it, and **under** the next one. Read that again.

At this point you are in the position shown in Fig. 1. Now turn the rope over as in Fig. 2. Take the remaining untucked strand (X) and tuck it as in Fig. 3.

Now continue, over and under, working to the left for three tucks. Trim off the ends, and the splice is complete. You can then pad the eye with hose pipe, or, in some cases make the loop round a metal eye.

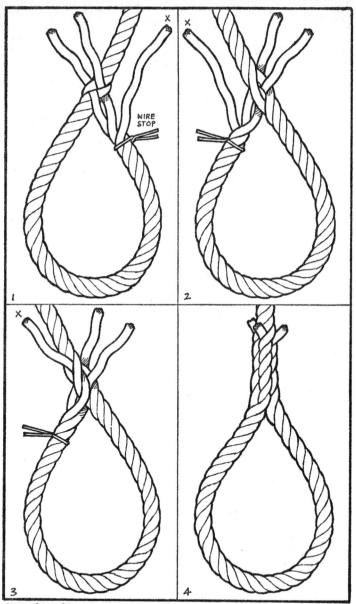

WIRE STOP

1

2

3

4

EYE SPLICE

SHORT SPLICE

Uses: For joining two ropes permanently. It is a lot stronger than any knot.

How to do it: Twist a piece of wire around the rope ends as in Fig. 1, to stop excessive unravelling, and then unlay the ends down to the stops.

Marry up the opposed strands until each strand lies between two others, and bring up to the stops, as in Fig. 2.

Take the left hand strands and stop them to the stranded part of the left hand rope (Fig. 3).

Remove stop from right hand rope. Then as before, take any loose strand and tuck over and under the strand in the right hand rope. Work to the left, taking the next (left) strand, and so on round, until you have put three tucks in each strand.

Then remove stop from left hand rope, and repeat, still working to the left.

Trim off the ends.

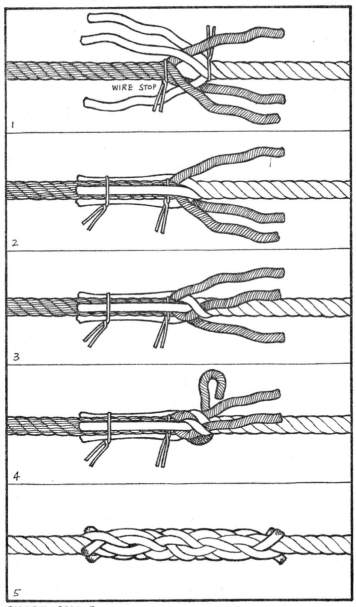

WIRE STOP

1

2

3

4

5

SHORT SPLICE